CW00542115

MUSIC & LIFE
REGGAE PROPHETS

Palmwine Sounds

RAFFIA PRESS

Copyright © 2024 Palmwine Publishing

All rights reserved. No part of this publication may be reproduced, distributed, or transmitted in any form or by any means, including photocopying, recording, or other electronic or mechanical methods, without the prior written permission of the publisher, except in the case of brief quotations embodied in critical reviews and certain other non-commercial uses permitted by copyright law.

Author- Palmwine Sounds

Illustrator- Kehinde Omotosho

ISBN- 978-978-784-731-2

Published by Raffia Press an Imprint of Palmwine Publishing

Illustrated By- Kehinde Omotosho

Linktree: https://linktr.ee/bbfpress

Publisher: Palmwine Publishing

Address: 1A Jos Road Bukuru, Plateau State, Nigeria.

ABOUT THE BOOK

"Music and Life: Reggae Prophets" delves into the influence of Rastafarianism on reggae. Rastafarianism, a faith, and cultural movement that originated in Jamaica in the 1930s, heavily influenced the lyrics and themes of reggae songs. The book explores the Rastafarian beliefs in unity, love, and social justice, and how these principles are reflected in the poetic nature of reggae music.

Throughout the book, the author highlights the key figures who played a significant role in shaping reggae music and its poetic message. These "Reggae Prophets" include legendary artists such as Bob Marley, Peter Tosh, and Burning Spear, among others. The author delves into their poetic techniques, the themes they explored in their lyrics, and the profound impact they had on the reggae movement.

THE RASTA MAN

The rasta man can't be understood.
The rasta man puts Jah first.
The rasta man's religion is love.
The rasta man is a peaceful man.
The rasta man strides with a hint of violence.
The rasta man is not judgemental.
The rasta man stands for truths and rights.
The rasta man prays and smiles problems away.
The rasta man treat females as queens and princesses.
The rasta man is inquisitive by nature.
The rasta man always protects his own.
The rasta man smokes his herb in peace.
The rasta man is on the vital ital diet.
The rasta man loves the little adults.
The rasta man stands for truths and rights.
The rasta man chants and sings with the Nyabinghi.
The rasta man appreciates bass rhythms.
The rasta man listens to reggae prophets.

HERB BE FREE

The International herb
Marimarijuana
The weed, Mary Jane
Ganja, Chronic.

Enjoyed by Jarheads.
Help Sadhus meditate.
Buddhist uses as medication.
Gives prophets inspiration in music.

THE BUSH DOCTOR

Legalise it and Tosh would patronise it.
Wanted, dread or alive, for herb.
Bomboclat!!!!!!!!!! Rasclat!!!!!!!!!
Natty arrested, for antidepressant.
Bald head arrested, for medication.
The good leaf hurts no one.
Cigarettes be legal but herb be illegal?

Peter Tosh

DUBE

Shotgun to the chest,
Grandmother son dead.

Babylon has taken another rasta,
Hundreds more shall keep the flame.

On till all colours are one,
The rasta men shall tread on.

Lucky Philip Dube

CULTURE

Prophets in the chancel.
Playing skilfully with angels.
The band calls, angels respond.

Jacob's favourite son leads.
Worshipping Jah Rastafari,
While preaching on truth and rights.

Joseph Hill

BOB

Game is tied
The final minute
Bob gets the ball
With Jah's strength
He dribbles the ball
He shoots, heading to post
The ball deflects off the bar
Hits Bob on the head
Natty dreadlocks unravel
Three little birds' circle.

In the hospital
Nurses and doctor surround
Bob shares his dream
He was in an English farm
Picking berries for jam
He wailed in delight
I was jamming!!!!

Robert Nesta Marley

Robert Nesta Marley

THE MADMAN

I am a madman.
I am a badman.
I am a court case.

Babylonians shall be upset.
Violence shall chase them.
As long as Scratch's dub is played.

Lee "Scratch" Perry

ROMEO

Have you heard the story?
About Prophet Romeo,
Who wore an iron shirt,
And chased satan out of earth.
He did not stop there,
He then put on an iron space suit,
Picked up a shotgun that fires lightning,
Chased him to the edge of the universe.

Max Romeo

JERUSALEM/ZION

Forward to Zion we match.
Prophet Blondy leads the way.
Muslim, Christians, Jews, Rasta...
All welcome to the match.

Leaving behind all the wicked ones
Leaving Babylonians behind
We shall beat drums.
Accompanied by bass to Jah.

Alpha Blondy

GARVEY DUB

Spear the Dub controller.
The drums shouts Marcus,
The bass plays Garvey.

The Pan-African dub plays.
The girls whine to it,
As the message plays.

Burning Spear

THE MISSIONARY JOURNEY

With the blessing of Marcus Garvey,
Reggae must be spread internationally.
From the heart of Jamaica,
The Prophets shall board the Black Star Liner.
Like the Sons of Thunder, the tread on,
Spreading the ideology.

First stop to Africa.

Pay homage to our Emperor,
Ethiopia, we go.
Restock on herb in Shashamane.

Visit Lucky Dube in South Africa.
Visit Alpha Blondy in Ivory Coast.
Visit Daddy Showkey in Nigeria.

Over to Europe.

Smoke kaya in Buckingham Palace.
The stages of One Love Festival, Reggae Land, Simmer
down Festival, Positive Vibration and Notting Hill Carnival
shall become the pulpit.

The prophets where perplexed,
Herb be legal in Amsterdam.
The Two Sevens festival we shall clash.
Gifted different strains to fuel the journey.

We skank on over to Asia.

The prophets tread around Chiney walls.
Preach at the Highest Mountain festival.
Over to India to meditate with the Sadhus.

We hop on over to Australia.

The prophets went on a Safari.
The heat of the sun bleached our locks.
Our Herb be smoking on its own.

This righteous ship we ride to the Americas.

Welcomed like soldiers after war in USA.
The Prophets Vs the Brazilian Football team
Finally resting in Canada with a zoot in hand.

Marcus Mosiah Garvey

CHANT UP NYABINGI!

Let chalice be blazed!
And Jah be praised.

The rasta men in a drum circle
The heartbeat rhythms begin.

Chant up Jah!
Chant down Satan.

Chant up Zion!
Chant down Babylon.

Chant up one love!
Chant down disunity.

Chant up happiness!
Chant down Downpression.

Chant up reggae prophets!
Chant down wicked men.

The rasta men shall chant till Jericho's walls crumble.
Smoke from the herb shall blind all defenders.

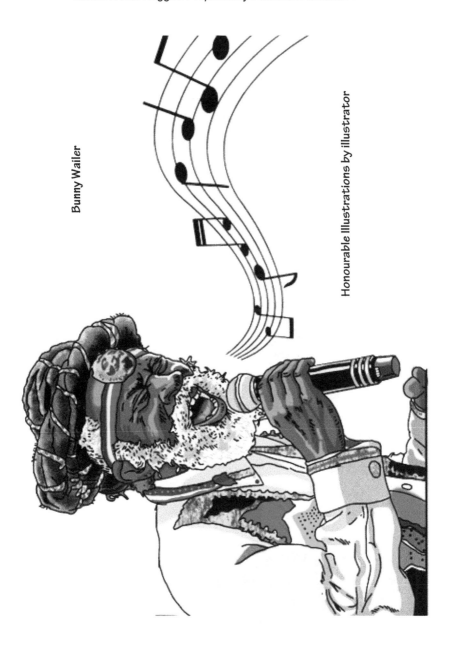

Bunny Wailer

Honourable Illustrations by illustrator

Jimmy Cliff

Honourable Illustrations by illustrator

Notes

'Thay may peper and solt it as they plese'.
- Timothy Dexter

Milton Keynes UK
Ingram Content Group UK Ltd.
UKHW050427230324
439897UK00009B/21